SALAMANDERS

CREEPY CRAWLERS

Lynn Stone

The Rourke Book Co., Inc.
Vero Beach, Florida 32964

PHOTO CREDITS
Title page, pages 7 and 15 © Breck P. Kent;
pages 4 and 18 © James P. Rowan;
Cover and pages 8, 10, 12, 13, 17, 21 © Lynn M. Stone

Library of Congress Cataloging-in-Publication Data

Stone, Lynn M.
    Salamanders / by Lynn M. Stone.
        p. cm. — (Creepy crawlers)
    Includes index.
    Summary: Presents information about this amphibian most commonly found in North and South America, describes how it looks, how it lives, and how it relates with people.
    ISBN 1-55916-164-7
    1. Salamanders—Juvenile literature. [1. Salamanders.]
I. Title II. Series: Stone, Lynn M.   Creepy crawlers
QL 668.C2S82   1995
597.6'5—dc20   95–16558
                                                       CIP
                                                       AC

Printed in the USA

TABLE OF CONTENTS

SALAMANDERS

When it comes to squiggly creatures, some of the salamanders are the squiggliest! Most salamanders feel like slimy bags of jelly.

In fact, salamanders are **amphibians** (am FIB ee enz), like frogs and toads. Amphibians need plenty of moisture to stay alive. It's no wonder, then, that they're slimy.

The best salamander **habitat** (HAB uh tat), or homeland, is in the Americas—North and South. More kinds of salamanders live in North and South America than in the whole rest of the world.

This marbled salamander, like other land salamanders, needs to stay moist

WHAT SALAMANDERS LOOK LIKE

Most salamanders, with their four legs and their long tails, look like wet, smooth-skinned lizards. They're not related to lizards, however. Lizards are reptiles. They're covered with scales and they have claws on their four feet. Salamanders are clawless, although not toothless.

The smallest salamanders in North America are about two inches long. The largest, called an amphiuma, is nearly four feet long. The world's biggest salamander is the five-foot long Japanese salamander.

Colorful cave salamander shows the smooth, moist skin of its tribe

WHERE SALAMANDERS LIVE

North American salamanders live throughout the United States and in parts of Southern Canada. Most species live in the Southeast.

The best places to find salamanders are wet woodlands, brooks, ponds, and swamps.

As adults, most salamanders breathe air and live on land. They hide under stones, logs, and leaves. Some **species** (SPEE sheez), or kinds, live in caves.

Aquatic (uh KWAHT ihk) salamanders, the kinds that live entirely in water, are eel-like creatures. They breathe through gills and live in bodies of fresh water.

The lungless dusky salamander lives near mountain brooks

HOW SALAMANDERS LIVE

Salamanders follow a basic rule for survival: Moisture is a must.

Salamanders rarely travel far from water, and they are largely **nocturnal** (nahk TUR nul)—animals of the night. Prowling in the coolness of the night helps salamanders save the moisture in their bodies.

Some of the land-based salamanders breathe through lungs. Others are lungless. These species of salamanders breathe through moist skin and the lining of the mouth.

The ozark blind cave salamanders have lived in the moist darkness of caves for so long that their eyes are sightless

Salamanders are meat-eaters, and worm meat is neat if you're a tiger salamander

Common red-backed salamander lives in the woodland of northern North America

KINDS OF SALAMANDERS

About 350 kinds of salamanders live worldwide. The number of species will increase as scientists continue to find "new" species.

Canada and the United States have about 115 kinds of salamanders. They belong to seven different groups.

Many groups have curious names, like newt, siren, mudpuppy, and waterdog. People used to believe that the aquatic waterdogs could bark. Actually, salamanders are nearly voiceless.

Yonahlossee salamander of southern Appalachian Mountains is one of about 115 kinds of salamanders north of Mexico

SALAMANDER COUSINS

The salamander's cousins are other amphibians: frogs and toads.

"Amphibia" means life in land and water. Nearly all frogs, toads, and salamanders spend some time in water and on land.

Amphibians share other likenesses with each other. Amphibian skin is bumpy sometimes, but it's always soft and without hair or scales. Amphibian eggs are laid in jellylike globs, usually in water.

The broken-striped newt belongs to one of the seven salamander groups found in North America

YOUNG SALAMANDERS

Most young salamanders begin life in water. They're called **larvas** (LAR vuhz), and they breathe through gills, like fish.

Some salamander species quickly change from water-breathing larvas into air-breathing adults. Other species, however, may remain in the larval stage for years.

As adults, land salamanders return to water to lay their eggs, usually in the spring. During this time, huge numbers of salamanders may gather in pools and ponds.

A woodland salamander's larva leads an aquatic life before becoming an air-breathing adult

PREDATOR AND PREY

Salamanders live quiet, out-of-the-way lives, like woodland hermits. At feeding time, though, salamanders are not shy!

Salamanders are **predators** (PRED uh terz). They hunt and eat other living creatures, such as worms and insects. Larger salamanders catch fish, frogs, and small snakes.

Salamanders are also **prey** (PRAY), or food, for larger predators. Raccoons, snakes, herons, cranes, and even cougars like salamander snacks.

This sandhill crane jabbed the amphiuma a few times, then swallowed it whole

SALAMANDERS AND PEOPLE

People capture salamanders for pets and fish bait. Far worse for salamanders, however, is the loss of moist habitat. When wetlands are drained for homes and farms, salamanders disappear.

Seven species of salamanders in the United States are in danger of disappearing forever. Many other species live only in very small areas. If their homes disappear, so will these colorful, harmless amphibians.

Glossary

amphibian (am FIB ee en) — any one of a group of soft, moist-skinned animals that are usually born in water and usually become air-breathing land animals as adults; frogs, toads, and salamanders

aquatic (uh KWAHT ihk) — of or related to water, such as an aquatic flower

habitat (HAB uh tat) —the kind of place where an animal lives, such as a forest

larva (LAR vuh) — the stage of development between egg and adult in certain animals, such as salamanders and frogs

nocturnal (nahk TUR nul) — active at night

predator (PRED uh ter) — an animal that hunts another animal for food

prey (PRAY) — an animal that is hunted by another animal as food

species (SPEE sheez) — within a group of closely related animals, one certain kind, such as a *tiger* salamander

INDEX